Farewell Darth Vader:

A Philosopher's Simple Introduction to Basic Principles of 12 Step Recovery

Kevin Vader

DEDICATION

To all those who helped me through recovery. Family and friends whose support means more than you will ever know. To the Retreat, Into-Action Big Book study group, and all those I have met in Al-Anon and AA. I'm thankful for the many lessons I've learned and look forward to many more.

Please feel free to review, share comments, or ask questions about this book at Amazon.com (this book should be listed there).

CONTENTS

Chapter 1

INTRODUCTION

A few years ago I knew almost nothing about Alcoholics Anonymous (AA) or any of the other similar recovery programs for eating disorders, narcotics, gambling, sex addiction, codependency, etc. Like many others I knew there were 12 steps, that people attended meetings, and had a "higher power". It came as quite a surprise to me when I learned that the program of AA is really about learning a new way of life. As a philosopher who has formally studied perspectives on how one should live, I was pleasantly surprised by the insights of the AA program. I think the principles that underlie its framework for living can benefit everyone – even those (like me) who are not alcoholics, and even those who think their life is just fine.

My primary motive for writing this very short book is simple: I wanted some of my family and friends who know so little about 12 step programs to have a simple introduction. I also hope this short book might help a few who read it, or at least get them thinking about important issues in how to live. I am especially motivated to write something I could give to my children. When I was a teenager I wish I had a guide like this. Of course, as a teenager I probably would have read it only if forced. Then I would have dismissed it as babbling nonsense from an old fool because that is what I did with just about everything when I was younger.

This book is not a guide on how to work the 12 step program. I will not even go through the steps. Instead I will try to describe the underlying principles in 12 step recovery programs, focusing on Alcoholics Anonymous which was the first program. These principles come from the way of life the program of AA describes in its central texts, especially the *Big Book of Alcoholics Anonymous* (BB) and the *Twelve Steps and Twelve Traditions* (12&12).

These central texts of AA are wonderful, and I highly recommend them. But I also know after my first reading of these texts, I barely scratched the surface in understanding them. It was only with the help of others in AA and Al-Anon, with their experience and insights, that I really began to unpack the rich content and gain a deeper understanding of the way of life these texts describe. And of course I still have much to learn, from others and also from practicing recovery in real life. For it is one thing to intellectually understand these principles of recovery, but another to really live them. And it is by living them that I have come to deepen my understanding.

What follows is my interpretation and introduction to some of the essential principles and teachings of the AA program. It is only meant to be a starting point or guideline. I have not found much material that focused specifically on the principles of AA, so I welcome a deeper discussion of these principles.

To help foster discussion, I have done my best to focus on central/basic underlying principles of living that can be applied by anyone, including atheists. These principles, as I develop them, do not require you to believe in God. Nor do they require worldviews like those in Zen or other Eastern Religions. Religious views can certainly supplement the principles I discuss. And I will even briefly touch upon how familiar ideas of recovery like "being God-reliant" can be useful, instructive, and powerful enhancements to the basic principles I discuss. But my focus will be on principles for everyone, even those who do not believe in God. In addition, I want to unpack what phrases like "God-reliant" really mean in the practice of daily living. Again, these basic principles I discuss are only a starting point. I strongly believe each person must find their way through recovery and life on their own, reanimating these basic principles for themselves, adding color, content, and significant details given their unique beliefs and religious background, personal history, and social context.

Chapter 2 discusses the principles of 12 step recovery. It is my attempt to present the basic principles in a short and simple way. I forced my intelligent teenage daughter to read this chapter, and confirm that it could be understood even by those with no background in recovery.

Chapter 3 describes how I came to understand and live the principles in my recovery. It is my personal story of strength and hope. This chapter is probably the easiest to read, and could even be read before the other chapters if desired. That said, I wrote chapter three with the intent to clarify and deepen the concepts of chapter two with specifics from my experience. Shared stories of recovery truly deepen our understanding, and remain a fundamental practice of recovery.

Finally, **Chapter 4** is the most philosophical. It is meant to be philosophy for everyone, and does not require any philosophy background. However, I doubt one can really appreciate this chapter without the conceptual introduction to the principles of recovery in Chapter 2. Chapter 4 examines these basic principles in relation to God, the Problem of Evil, Eastern Philosophy, and Virtue Ethics. If you don't know about any of these things, that's OK. No prior experience is required. This is not an academic book, but a simple introduction written by a simple no-nonsense philosopher.

Chapter 2

WHAT ARE THE BASIC PRINCIPLES OF 12 STEP RECOVERY?

Consumers of Happiness No More

Much of our lives we are taught that happiness is something we get. It's a part of our culture. Advertising, movies, and other social influences try to convince us that we might be happy if we could have a nice house or car, maybe some new jeans or shoes. They can also suggest less materialistic ways about finding happiness – maybe if I lose weight, get a new job, find true love, become more popular, or achieve amazing success. We learn to think of ourselves as consumers of happiness. If only we had this and maybe that, we would be happy.

No matter how many pieces of happiness we acquire, there is always more. And we wonder how those who have the most, still can be unhappy. The problem is that there is much more involved in happiness, and in a good life, than what we acquire. The focus of 12 step recovery is not on having, but being. Another way to say this is that it is about what is inside of us: in our attitudes, perspectives, and motives – in how we live, not what we have. Learning this way of life is not a simple decision one makes like buying new jeans. Instead it is a process that one continues to develop and actively works to maintain.

There is much about this process that is specific to each individual, and this is what I mean by each person finding their own way.

The two primary texts of AA are the *Big Book of Alcoholics Anonymous* (BB) and the *Twelve Steps and Twelve Traditions* (12&12). It was a surprise to me when I learned these texts teach us that alcohol is not really the problem for alcoholics. The fundamental problem is in how we live. Alcohol is a kind of solution to the problem. It's a bad solution, one that avoids the fundamental problem inside oneself, and typically deepens the problem even more. It's a solution that finds contentment outside, and specifically from substances.

Substances can be a way to cope with problems or difficult emotions, to deal with lifelong resentments or uncertainty about the future. No matter how miserable one might be – social outcast, no money, no friends, no family, raging emotions – one can still find "happiness" by drinking alcohol. And even if someone has a lot of success – well, they can always have more, and using substances can make life just that much more "fun and enjoyable". Many successful celebrities and sports stars know this all too well.

The fundamental problem, according to these AA texts, is in the way we approach life. More specifically, there are two big problems in the way alcoholics (and I suggest many others) live: **self-centeredness** and **dishonesty**. These are not the only two obstacles, but these are certainly two of the biggest obstacles.

Selfishness – self-centeredness! That we think is the root of our troubles. (BB pg. 62)

The basic texts of AA have many passages about self-centeredness. When I first read these passages I dismissed them applying to me. After all, I typically put others before me.

I gave to my kids, my wife, and my coworkers. Sure, most of them might be self-centered, not me.

One of the most important learnings for me during recovery was a much deeper understanding of self-centeredness. And yes, even though I gave quite a bit to others, I learned that I was indeed self-centered in ways I had never thought of, never realized. In the next section I will begin describing these insights into self-centeredness. After that, I will discuss dishonesty.

Self-Centered Attitudes - Letting Go of Resentment and Fear

As a kid, I grew up watching *Star Wars*. I understood how anger and hate could lead one to the dark side. Darth Vader clearly had anger management issues, and most would agree he is not a happy person. But Yoda also talks about fear. For instance I wondered what Yoda meant when he said that "Fear is the path to the dark side. Fear leads to anger...." While not intended to do so, AA gives rich insight into what Yoda means. Not only does AA link resentment and fear, it weaves them together as forms of self-centeredness that lead us toward the dark side, and prevent us from living well - from a flourishing meaningful life.

AA members typically do three kinds of "moral inventory": resentment, fear, and sex. I won't address sex here. In addition they can also do an inventory of "Harms to Others". These inventories are the core of Step 4: "Made a searching and fearless moral inventory of ourselves". These inventories are actual worksheets one often does with a mentor or sponsor, and there are specific examples of these moral inventories in the Big Book. It is quite clear, according to AA texts, that resentment and fear are two of the most significant obstacles to sobriety, serenity, and a fulfilling life. The next sections will describe how resentment and fear are symptoms of our self-centeredness, how they imprison us, and how we can free ourselves from them to build a better life.

Resentment

Resentment is the "number one" offender. It destroys more alcoholics than anything else. (BB 64)

It is plain that a life which includes deep resentment leads only to futility and unhappiness. (BB 66)

One way I like to understand resentment is as an attitude I have toward things in the past. It's an attitude I have about how things in the past did not go "right". Often what we mean when we say things did not go "right" is that they did not go the way "I wanted". For example, maybe I wanted a promotion I did not get, or maybe my chances for my dream house went to a higher bidder. When it is simply a matter of things not going MY WAY it is very obvious how this can be self-centered.

In some cases, things not going right can be more than things not going my way. It may be that things not only did not go my way, but they did not go the way they "should" have gone, perhaps if life were fair. Is it really fair that I got cancer, that my parents abandoned me, that others bully or abuse me, that an accident paralyzed me, that my spouse had affairs, that my best friend betrayed me, that my child died? Another way of putting this is that I did not deserve this kind of misfortune.

So to summarize things in the past did not go MY WAY, or perhaps even the WAY THEY SHOULD. The next step is my **response** to that past misfortune. My response, one that I choose, can be an attitude of resentment where I cling to that past not going right and view myself as a victim. In contrast, AA teaches us to **ACCEPT** that things do not always go MY WAY or even THE WAY THEY SHOULD.

Now before my introduction to AA I was not a fan of "acceptance". I thought it was a word for quitters. But along the way I learned one important clarification: accepting things do not always go my way or even the way they should does not prevent me from taking actions. Accepting does not mean we should just roll over and play dead - that we should allow injustice to continue, stay in abusive relationships, or do nothing about cancer. Indeed we should certainly work for positive change, for improving our life and that of others. It is vitally important to know that I can still take action whether I am resentful or not – what changes is my perspective, my attitude, and my motives for acting. I will touch on these changes next.

The change in perspective is that things do not always go right, and we cannot change the past. It is too bad that things do not always go right, but that is the way it is. Second, we choose to not hold onto the attitude of anger. We learn (over time) to let that anger go, rather than playing it over in our heads, choosing and building an attitude of resentment. It's not forced forgiveness, but openly accepting that whatever ticked me off happened to me and that's a part of my life. So we no longer remain in a state of self-pity. We no longer view ourselves as victims. Instead, we learn from the past and move on, letting go of our anger toward that past, our hostile thoughts and feelings about what I deserved. This is the shift in perspective and attitude.

Of course, changing our attitude can also change our motives and actions. With an attitude of resentment, a common reaction, one perhaps glorified in our culture is revenge. Fired by a burning resentment, we plot the demise of our enemies, and show the world that nobody messes with ME. In contrast, if you really let go of your resentment, you will not seek revenge. You may decide to sever a friendship, or be more careful, or some other action to improve the situation. But your actions will not be motivated by a desire for revenge – instead they will be motivated by a desire to improve situations or help people. It is a positive motive for change, not a negative motive for revenge. We will circle back to this in the next section when we talk about motives and behaviors.

Resentment is often directed toward other people or unfair situations, but I can also be the source of resentment for myself: "I messed up and I hate myself". One common way this self-resentment shows itself is as a lack of self-value or self-esteem. I'm not worthy, I'm a bad person, I have no purpose, etc. There are many reasons we might resent ourselves. It might be because we were told we were bad, or because we feel like failures. A very common reason for resenting ourselves is our mistakes.

We all make mistakes, doing things that hurt ourselves or others. AA teaches us it is crucial to accept responsibility for our mistakes, and make amends. In fact, Step 8 is devoted to this: "Made a list of all persons we had harmed, and became willing to make amends to them all". It is common knowledge in AA that this list of people harmed, and to whom one makes amends, should most likely include oneself. It is vitally important that we do not hold on to our mistakes, wallowing in shame and guilt, seeing ourselves as losers who deserve nothing. We all have regrets, we all are human and imperfect, but we need to learn from mistakes and move on, not cling to them in perpetual self-loathing. This is a very important change in our perspective and attitude. Resentment toward ourselves is not helpful for anyone and can be even more damaging to a flourishing meaningful life than resentment toward others.

Again, the bigger lesson is that we should accept that things do not always go MY WAY or even THE WAY THEY SHOULD. The past is filled with mistakes and unfairness. We should acknowledge our part, our mistakes, and make amends if needed. Then we should learn from the past to shape the future, and move on. Holding onto anger about the past will not change the past. In fact, it most likely only changes you – eating you up inside, spreading darkness within you, while others who harmed you may not even care. We decide to let go, to free ourselves from the chains of resentment by which we imprison ourselves.

Much of the discussion here will become even clearer in the next section where we discuss an issue with many parallels to resentment: the obstacle of fear.

Fear (and More Resentment)

Fear covers a lot of territory, and serves a useful purpose. It helps prevent us from doing things that might hurt us like playing with poisonous snakes, jumping from high places, or sleeping on a railroad track. We certainly want to avoid injury or death when possible.

Now the examples of fear above are not what typically get discussed in AA inventories. Typically the fears are more general and persistent fears about what our lives will be like, as well as others we care about. My wife might leave me, my child is struggling with addiction, a loved one might die, my heart might be broken, my friends might betray me.

In all of these cases, fear draws our attention to something worth noticing about the future. It is OK and even desirable to prepare and try to influence the future. We should plan a hike to avoid dangerous snakes and treacherous cliffs. Likewise, it is fine to dream about what we might do with our lives, about how we can make our lives and the world a better place. We should help prepare our children to be successful, and think about our finances. But we should also accept that our dreams may not come true - that mistakes and misfortunes are most likely a part of our future, just as they are in our past. The most we can do is **influence** the future, **not dictate** it.

Just as we saw with resentment, accepting this does not prevent me from taking actions or planning. Nobody should just roll over and play dead. What changes is my attitude. It's an attitude of open-mindedness toward the future.

Open-mindedness can be tough. It means we recognize our limited power to influence outcomes. So it requires a degree of humility. The young Darth Vader had a real problem with this. He had his own ideas about what the outcome should be, and he was willing to embrace the dark side to have more control over his future. Humility was something he left behind in his quest for power, to rule the galaxy and conquer death.

Open-mindedness means we not only recognize our limited power, but *accept* that uncertainty. Most people don't want to accept this uncertainty, or to put it more bluntly, hear that their dreams might not come true. Like Darth Vader, it is natural for my self-centeredness to hold on to what I planned: my desires, my agenda, my dreams for the future. It's sad that there are no guarantees. Movies and novels tell countless stories about how in the end dreams really do come true. These happy movies often reinforce the assumption that contentment comes from outside, from achieving dreams. Instead we should learn to find contentment in who we are, from living our lives the best way we can today. The dreams may or may not come true. It's not what we acquire -- prestige, romance, success, but who we are and how we live. It's about being our best today, while accepting that we all make mistakes and life is uncertain.

Being open-minded about our journey of life does not mean despair; it is not resignation to a future of failures. What we need to cultivate is a positive sense of open-mindedness – one where it becomes a spirit of discovery and hope, of challenges and opportunities for growth. One thing that helps me is to ask myself what lessons I might learn, and to open myself to learning them. And by all means it is essential to strive, to do our best whatever the outcome. What happens after that is beyond our control.

We may find our lives are turning out very differently from the way we dreamt they would be, but that this very different life we have is a wonderful life after all. There are many great stories about this. I recently watched the movie "Soul Surfer". Based on a true story it tells about a young surfer who lost her arm to a shark, and thought her surfing career was over. Her life had been ruined, or so she thought. Instead, she developed a new life, inspiring many others with handicaps. There are similar stories in AA about how people have transformed their lives from drunks who lost nearly everything and then became role models living amazing lives helping others. None of these people dreamt they would be in AA, and that their life would involve helping other drunks, but it's a life they cherish. You never know who you might be able to help in life, what positive influence you might have, what the future has in store for you.

For now, I want to emphasize the open-minded attitude of accepting the journey of life. It's an adventure that may not always be what we expect or dream about, a journey that may be fraught with failures or filled with successes. But it's a journey that we are open to, because we have surrendered that self-centeredness about what I deserved in the past (and resent that I did not get) or I deserve in the future (and fear I may lose or not get). It's a journey where achieving our agendas, our dreams, our fair rewards, is replaced with doing our very best, accepting what we cannot change, and embracing open-mindedness, hope, and courage in the midst of uncertainty.

More on Accepting with Comments on God

The idea of "accepting what we cannot change" is a widely known phrase in the serenity prayer typically recited at the end of most AA meetings:

> God, Grant me the serenity to accept the things I cannot change
> The courage to change the things I can
> And the wisdom to know the difference

This is a wonderful prayer which emphasizes accepting what cannot be changed, while also recognizing the importance of courage. One small aside is that philosophers like to distinguish between cannot, can, and should. Knowing the difference between these three can be difficult, and is the subject of much philosophical discussion. So I modified the serenity prayer above to this more philosophically accurate one:

> Grant me the *humility* and *serenity* to accept the things I
> cannot change,
> The *honesty* and *insight* to know what I can change,
> The *wisdom* and *courage* to change the things I should

The serenity prayer is a request to God, and it is certainly important to acknowledge that God, or the more neutral term Higher Power, is part of the AA tradition. Historically AA was initially influenced by the Oxford Group. This was a group of Christians who emphasized the importance of serving God in our everyday life, doing God's will and trusting in Him. And indeed one way to clarify what I have described here is that our new way of life comes from doing God's will, not ours. My focus is on the practical insights of AA, so I don't want to address the very big issue of God here. However, I do think the idea of taking my life as a servant to a loving God who cares for us is a very instructive and historically justified way to describe underlying principles of recovery.

Briefly, one common way the God approach can be applied is if we think that God may have very different plans for our lives than we do. My big ego with its own ideas about what my life should be like (in the past or future) needs to let go and be open to what God has planned for me. This is one way to think of open-mindedness toward the future and letting go of resentments toward the past.

> God was going to be our Director. He is the Principal;
> we are His agents.... Being all powerful, he provided
> what we needed, if we kept close to Him and
> performed His work well. (BB 84-85)

In this view, my life is about seeking and doing God's will, with my life bearing witness to His light and love in all that I do. What happens beyond that is outside human control, in the hands of God. The measure of success is in how well we serve God, not what we have. You may not have a nice car or a supportive family. You may not have the life you expected, but you rejoice and find fulfillment in serving God. This illustrates the point of saying that for us there is only the trying, that success is measured by how we live, not the outcome.

> God, I offer myself to Thee -- to build with me and to do with me as Thou wilt. Relieve me of the bondage of self, that I may better do Thy will. Take away my difficulties, that victory over them may bear witness to those I would help of Thy Power, Thy Love, and Thy Way of life. May I do Thy will always! (BB 63)

> Every day is a day when we must carry the vision of God's will into all of our activities. "How can I best serve Thee – Thy will (not mine) be done" (BB 85)

As a servant of God, one practices humility (which I will discuss later), living the kind of life God wants you to live, which may differ from the one you expected. It's not about your agenda, but God's. Step 11 makes this very clear when it emphasizes "praying only for knowledge of His will for us and the power to carry that out". The Big Book clearly tells us: "We are careful never to pray for our own selfish ends" (BB 87). It is about serving God, not using Him as a vending machine to get what we want. We are open to the life God has in mind for us – a perfect example of open-mindedness.

There is no doubt these kinds of passages about God permeate the Big Book and many AA meetings. I think the idea of joyfully serving a loving omnipotent God is probably the easiest way to approach the principles of AA. At the same time there are significant groups of AA members who do not believe in God, and take their Higher Power to be the principles of AA, Right Living, Nature, or the Tao. As I mentioned before, there are many ways to adopt the principles of AA into one's life given one's specific background. So I am deliberately trying to stay clear of the very big issue of God, and focus on the underlying principles.

However we get there, the underlying insight in this section is that we should accept things do not always go MY WAY or maybe even THE WAY THEY SHOULD. This applies to the past (resentments) and to the future (fear). Letting go of these also means letting go of self-pity, of seeing ourselves as victims. We also accept that we cannot change the past or dictate the future. This is the fundamental principle of letting go.

Some people like to use phrases like detachment for this. I think this is fine, as long as that detachment is a healthy independence, not cold or uninvolved. I think it is important to engage life and embrace living. So rather than detachment I prefer to think of it as "not letting things get to you". We do our best, recognize we make mistakes, and accept that what happens beyond that is outside our control. We detach from the final outcome, from things going our way or even sometimes the way they should. So I prefer to use words like acceptance or letting go, while stressing that acceptance does not become inaction. We recognize our limited powers and accept what we cannot change, but we also need to honestly ask ourselves what we can and should change, and have the courage to try. Sounds a lot like the serenity prayer.

None of this means we will or even should be happy all the time. We all suffer – some more than others. We feel angry at injustice and cruelty. We worry about loved ones and ourselves, and we feel grief in the face of loss. We should not deny these feelings, or bottle them up. **But the key is that these emotions should not define who we are or how we live.** Instead, we let ourselves feel these emotions, come to accept our misfortunes and the uncertainty of our future, learn what we can, and move forward with our lives in a positive way. For us, there is only the trying, where success is measured by how we live, not the outcome.

While we cannot dictate outcomes, we can control how we respond to life's events. Of course, we can respond with resentment and fear that are all so familiar. But instead of just living in resentment we can learn to respond with love and compassion. Instead of living in fear we can learn to respond with courage and open-mindedness. This may take time. When we lose a loved one, we grieve, and this is what we should do. But eventually we let go of that grief and accept the loss. In the same way we feel anger and fear. These draw our attention to something, and we ask what actions we should take. But then, like grief, we should let go of anger and fear, and respond with love, compassion, courage, and open-mindedness. Learning to respond this way may not be easy, but it can be done, and with practice may become easier. I think truly great people in history (perhaps people like Gandhi, Mother Theresa, Martin Luther King, Buddha, and Jesus) have cultivated and embraced this form of response as a way of life.

Positive Attitudes: Freedom, Gratitude, and Living More in the Present

The previous section focused on letting go of our resentments and our desire to dictate the future, accepting things do not always go my way or the way they should. To really work, this acceptance must be something we really want to choose. It is not resignation or compliance. It is not something we do reluctantly, because we are supposed to, or because it will make us look good. It is something we really choose because we think our lives will be richer and better. We have to see that resentments and fears are really like chains that hold us prisoner. They close our minds to the opportunities around us, and drive us deeper into self-centeredness. They are obstacles to contentment, serenity, and a flourishing life. For theists they may be obstacles to letting God in your life.

The more we allow resentment and fear to rule our lives, the more we tend to view ourselves as victims. Letting go of resentment and fear frees us from our bondage to the role of victim and feelings of self-pity. Letting go of them frees our spirits. We accept the past and embrace the adventure of our future. We can live. It is truly liberating.

Letting go of resentment and fear also opens the door to genuine gratitude. The more I think about what I deserve (resentment or fear), the less grateful one tends to be. In fact, our list of what we deserve can easily grow, no matter how much we have. I can always deserve more. Letting go of those negative feelings about what one deserves opens ourselves to true gratitude. This is not a gratitude that is forced, but really felt. It is a gratitude that is genuine or true.

With resentment and fear we can spend much of our time on what we want/deserve in the *future* or did not get/deserve in the *past*. Really letting go of those not only fosters an attitude of gratitude, but brings us toward *today* in a positive way -- away from resentments toward yesterday and fears about tomorrow. So a common practice of AA is daily gratitude, along with living more in the present. It is amazing how much of our lives we can miss living by dwelling on the past or the future. Awareness and enjoyment of the moment - be it awe, wonder, appreciation, gratitude, laughter, sharing, or just simple engagement – is an important reminder for all of us. We don't want the present to get lost.

Freedom from chains of what we deserve, coupled with gratitude and seizing the present are building blocks toward serenity and meaningful flourishing lives. We build on those blocks with hope, a positive attitude, and maybe even a little laughter. While these make a great start, we also cultivate this new way of life with our actions and motivations, which we will turn to next.

Self-Centered Motives And Behaviors

One of the most famous lines from legendary American President John F Kennedy is:

Ask not what your country can do for you – ask what you can do for your country.

The idea was to spin people's motives completely around, from one of "taking" to one of "giving", from selfishness to helping. Of course, we can broaden JFK's insight to ask what we can do for our family, our friends, our community, indeed what we can do for the entire world, even those who are our enemies. Rather than being consumers looking for happiness in what the world can do for me, we find contentment in living as full a life as possible, trying to do what is right, giving and helping to make the world a better place.

The wisdom of the 12 step recovery goes even deeper into the nature of this giving. It stresses that the point is to give without expecting anything back. Another way of putting this is that it's not a matter of trading – where I help you so you might help me later. When I first began recovery I thought I was a giver. True enough, I gave a lot to my wife and children, and rarely put myself first. But inside me I expected something back – at the very least I expected praise from them. "Poor Kevin, how does he put up with that wife? He really is a saint. He's accomplished so much". In Al-Anon, I found many people with similar backgrounds. Givers they were, but often expecting some kind of outcome or non-tangible reward, like praise, pity, or both. What recovery teaches us is that one should give without expecting any specific outcome, even be it the praise of others.

If one gives expecting something in return that is looking for happiness outside. It is a kind of reward, and is really a way to feed our egos, however subtle or unconscious of this we might be. AA teaches us to find contentment within, and part of that involves learning to enjoy giving and helping. We don't give in order to get something back or out of compliance or because others are more important than us. The point is to enjoy being a giver.

The nature of freely giving extends to everyone, even our so called enemies. An often recommended practice in AA is to pray for one's enemies. The result of this is to transform one's hatred into respect and tolerance, into wishing the very best for everyone.

> Most of us sense that real tolerance of other people's shortcomings and viewpoints and a respect for their opinions are attitudes which make us more useful to others. (BB 19-20)

> If we have been thorough about our personal inventory, we have written down a lot. We have listed and analyzed our resentments. We have begun to comprehend their futility and their fatality. We have commenced to see their terrible destructiveness. We have begun to learn tolerance, patience and good will toward all men, even our enemies, for we look on them as sick people. (BB 70)

Everyone has faults. Some people may have them to an extreme degree. At the very least, we should wish the very best for them. In some cases we may even try to help them. This of course is also a very Christian message, consistent with the Oxford Group. To love one's enemies was a somewhat radical suggestion by Jesus. Recovery teaches that we should at least tolerate and respect our enemies, wish the best for them.

Of course, we may not get anything back from our enemies. And indeed, the same may happen for those we consider friends and family. We may try our best to help them only to watch them destroy themselves. In Al-Anon one learns that you cannot cure the alcoholic. We can't control what happens beyond our helping. The point is to focus on doing what is right, and in wishing the very best for everyone (friend or not). And we should do this because it is the way to a good life, not because we expect something back.

One point I need to emphasize is that our respect, tolerance, and love should not only go out to others – be they friend or foe – but also to ourselves. We should respect everyone, including ourselves. This means we should take time for ourselves to enjoy life. It also means we recognize that just like others, we too make mistakes. **And we should wish the very best for ourselves to learn and grow from our mistakes.** To do our very best to improve ourselves, to be more useful, more understanding, more helpful, to be better parents and better role models. It's never too late to start and never too late to improve. This is the gift of hope, a gift of love for ourselves, even in the darkest moments of despair.

There are some amazing stories in AA of people who have transformed their lives. These people tell stories about their past lives – in jail, stealing from friends, violent crimes, lying, betraying loved ones, bitter, depressed, self-loathing. It's remarkable to hear these stories in themselves, but even more so because of whom they are now. Their lives have been transformed into loving givers, amazing role models, who work in the trenches helping others one day at a time. In many ways it's easier for them to tolerate, respect, and love others, because they have been there. They have learned to let go of many resentments and fears, to accept the past and be open about the future. They don't expect rewards or praise or even results, they just do the very best they can to help others, and rejoice in the lives they can lead now.

All of this builds upon the attitudes in the previous section. Resentment and fear drive us further into self-centeredness. So we surrendered those self-centered attitudes about what I deserved in the past (and resent that I did not get) or I deserve in the future (and fear I may not get). In this section, we extended the surrender of self-centeredness through our motives and actions. We freely give without expecting back, we try our best to improve our lives and make the world a better place, and openly accept the journey of life. Our motives and actions reinforce our attitudes. In turn, our attitudes strengthen our motives and actions, and we can spiral upward, building meaningful lives of serenity, contentment, and purpose.

Rigorous Honesty

Lying is a part of our culture. Marital affairs are common. We laugh when people lie on television shows, we accept and perhaps expect our politicians to lie, and we are sometimes taught to lie in many sports. If a basketball player said, "Oh no ref, he didn't foul me" his coach would be furious. We often go further, encouraging athletes to pretend they are fouled. I would even argue that our judicial system is based on manipulating evidence and facts to win a case. Honesty can be lost, trumped by "what can I get away with?" This may be the best we can do with a legal system, but it's not rigorous honesty and it's a poor model of how to live our daily lives.

In addition to lying in our culture, philosophical argument can defend our lying ways. Do I tell someone they look fat if they ask? What if the truth has lots of negative consequences? What if a lie can save someone's life? With all this, it is no wonder that many of us just throw in the towel and lie our way through life whenever it suits us.

In contrast, AA holds itself as a program of rigorous honesty, including honesty with yourself and others. I don't think this means one can never lie. But I do think it is important to understand when dishonesty is really bad, and what rigorous honesty might look like. To do this, I think we must first turn to one's motives.

One of the key questions we should ask ourselves is "why did I lie"? Better yet, we should be asking this question before the lie, "why am I going to lie?" If one is lying to save someone's life or help someone, then the dishonesty may be all right. These are tricky cases. But if I am lying because I want to hide something I did or I want to make myself look better, or to get something I want - then these are selfish motives, and feed into self-centeredness. It means that I am looking outside to find contentment. I want others to think a certain way about me, or I want to get something. Not only am I looking outside for contentment, but I am also manipulating others to get it.

Answering the question "why am I going to lie?" requires self-honesty. I can make up a bunch of crap about it being the situation, or forced into it, or they don't understand or some other rationalization. As a philosopher I've even told myself that there is no truth in the world – it's all interpretation. This is all crap, and the reason I like the term "rigorous honesty" is because I have to be honest with myself and look hard at my motives. It's not always easy, but I try not to take the easy way out. So the first point is to really cut through the bull, look at your motives, and to avoid dishonesty for selfish reasons.

In addition to avoiding dishonesty, there is also a proactive side to honesty. The clearest example of this, emphasized in AA, is that we should admit when we have done something wrong. This applies even when no one asks us or accuses us – it is proactive, not responsive. The 8th step is focused on making amends – taking responsibility for my past and apologizing. This becomes a daily practice in the 10th step: "Continued to take personal inventory and when we were wrong promptly admitted it".

There are several benefits to adopting this practice of proactive honesty.

First, it makes us more humble. We are not perfect, and we acknowledge that. Yes this step toward humility is difficult, but important to really face ourselves. In addition the vulnerability from admitting wrong can make us seem more human, more endearing. Shared vulnerability is a large part of what happens among AA members, and it brings them closer together.

Second, it brings us closer to others. When we do something wrong and hide it, we distance ourselves from others. Secrets make us sick. Big secrets can make us very sick and feel very alone. We hide these secrets deep inside ourselves, and they gnaw away at us. They lower our self-esteem, and can become a constant source of worry. We think we can handle them, but we know all too well that "the truth will set you free".

Third, acting on this principle pushes us away from deliberate wrongs. If I know that I am going to admit my wrongdoing, then I am less likely to do wrong. **Fourth**, when I admit my wrongs I am at the very least holding myself accountable for my actions. Here is what I did, and it was wrong. Accountability is a part of honesty, and embedded in the 10th step. **Finally**, proactive honesty forces us to confront our character defects, to make us aware of them, which is the first step toward learning and improving ourselves.

Rigorous honesty also includes self-honesty. We humans have a remarkable skill at telling ourselves lies. We can hide things from ourselves. We can hide our fears and resentments. We can make up stories about why we are worthless, or how we really don't have a problem, or how we didn't really do anything wrong. I know for many years that I liked to think I was never wrong. There was always someone or something else to blame for my mistakes. When we practice rigorous honesty with ourselves and others we become truly authentic. Failing to do that is an invitation to being divided by secrets, to feeling shame, personal discord and discontent.

I believe what I have outlined here are fundamental parts of AA's teachings about honesty. Others may want to take honesty still further. As I mentioned earlier, each person brings their unique histories and viewpoints to forge their own path. I have tried to lay down what I think are some basic essentials: avoiding dishonesty for selfish reasons, proactively admitting when we are wrong, and rigorous self-honesty. For me, these aspects of honesty are already very difficult to execute, but very rewarding. This kind of honesty helps make it much easier to live with oneself. It builds a sense of honor, trustworthiness, and authenticity. It also helps bring contentment, knowing that you are not lying to hide things or make yourself look better, that you are not self-centered, and that you proactively admit when you are wrong.

One of the concrete practices recommended in AA is a 10th step inventory every night.

> When we retire at night, we constructively review our day. Were we resentful, selfish, dishonest, or afraid? Do we owe an apology? Have we kept something to ourselves which should be discussed with another person at once? Were we kind and loving toward all? What could we have done better? Were we thinking of ourselves most of the time? Or were we thinking of what we could do for others, of what we could pack into the stream of life? (BB 86)

Here is one place where the Big Book says it wants to not be vague, and give "some definite and valuable suggestions". It begins by mentioning the web of self-centeredness, dishonesty, resentment, and fear. It addresses dishonesty by asking if we owe an apology (admitting our wrong) or if we are hiding something to ourselves. One helpful hint: if you are hiding something it is probably not good. Then the passage moves on to address letting go of self-centeredness, asking how we could improve ourselves and help others, to be kind and loving toward all. Finally I think it is important to mention the last sentence, about what we could pack into the stream of life. For me, this is about "seizing the day". This does not mean we have to run ourselves ragged, but we certainly want to avoid idle sulking and laziness. Instead, we want to look for opportunities to be productive, to share and celebrate, to help, and to really live, bringing a positive attitude into our daily life.

Conclusion: Surrender And Humility

AA is known as a program of surrender. Unlike many surrenders, this surrender must be freely chosen, without reluctance or force. It is something we want in order to live a satisfying and flourishing life. At the core of this surrender is the surrender of self-centeredness, which we can also call ego deflation, or humility. Chapter 7 of the *Twelve Steps and Twelve Traditions* is devoted to humility, and it clearly emphasizes how important it is to seek and learn true humility. Humility is in fact the foundation principle of each step.

> Indeed, the attainment of greater humility is the foundation principle of each of A.A.'s Twelve Steps. For without some degree of humility, no alcoholic can stay sober at all. Nearly all A.A.'s have found, too, that unless they develop much more of this precious quality than may be required just for sobriety, they still haven't much chance of becoming truly happy. (12&12, pg. 70)

Humility has a bad wrap (at least in the West), but true humility is not a humility of shame and guilt, of thinking we are worthless failures. It is recognizing our fallibility, and that of others. It's refusing to live in fear, putting aside my demands about how life should be, and opening ourselves to the unknown journey of life. It's letting go of resentments about what I deserved in the past, and learning what I can from them. It's bringing the positive attitude that is grateful for a glass half full (vs. half empty), sees hope in the future, and finds ways to celebrate life.

True humility is not a humility of weakness, where our actions are useless. We recognize our actions influence outcomes, but we are not omnipotent Gods who can dictate outcomes. Our actions are those of a giver trying to make ourselves and the world a better place rather than a taker always seeking more. Instead of asking what the world can do for me, we ask what we can do to make the world a better place. We lead lives of respect and love for everyone. We avoid manipulating others by dishonesty, and seek that inner harmony which comes from leading authentic honest lives as unconditional givers. We have the courage to admit and amend our wrongs, to put aside our selfish interests, and try our very best to shine light and love amidst darkness, and fearlessly do what is right.

The chart below shows one way to visualize these basic principles. At the center is the surrender of self-centeredness, which I call true humility. This humility involves a change in our attitudes, perspective, and motives/behaviors shown by the circle surrounding the core. Outside each part of the circle are the principles that describe the change in our attitudes, perspective, and motives/behaviors.

For example, the attitude that flows from surrendering self-centeredness is one of "Not Demanding Life Go My Way". This includes letting go of fear, resentment, and its relative self-pity. It means opening myself to the journey of life, and building acceptance of what we cannot change, being grateful for what we have, having courage to learn from the past and change what we should, and embracing the positive attitude of hope.

This true humility and the principles associated with it, to really work, must be something we seek, practice, and build into our lives. We must try to get completely away from any reluctance, resignation, or compliance – it is something we really choose to foster in ourselves to grow and flourish.

> To get away completely away from our aversion to the idea of being humble, to gain a vision of humility as the avenue to true freedom of the human spirit, to be willing to work for humility to be something desired for itself, takes most of us a long, long time. A whole lifetime geared to self-centeredness cannot be set in reverse all at once. (12&12, Pg. 73)

The surrender of self-centeredness and the corresponding change in perspectives, attitudes, and motives is an internal change in how we approach our life. This can be called a "psychic change" (BB Silkworth) or a "spiritual awakening" (Step 12), depending upon your personal preference.

I have no problem at all with calling the 12 step program a spiritual program. First, the program is a focus on our attitudes, motives, perspectives, and behaviors – these are spiritual or psychic, not material. We have an inner life. Of course, we also have an outer life of money, relationships, and material things. The focus of the 12 step program is on changes to the inner life. It is not a program designed to make you materially wealthy or achieve success. Its focus on the inner life makes it a spiritual program rather than material. That said, the external life is a place for us to practice and develop our ability to live by these principles. Relationships are a fundamental way to learn and practice treating all with respect, coming from a place of love and courage, rather than resentment or fear.

Second, the program emphasizes living in accordance with principles that one would typically call spiritual principles: surrendering self-centeredness, humility, letting go of resentment and fear, open-mindedness about the future, hope, courage, gratitude, acceptance, helping others without rewards, and rigorous honesty. These principles may or may not help you find material success. But they are the same kinds of principles one finds in many spiritual traditions or religions. Living according to these spiritual principles, one could be a Taoist, Muslim, Christian, Jew, or Buddhist, as well as many other religions. Any of these religions can supplement the basic principles here, in a way that is unique to each person's culture and history.

Third, the underlying principle of humility requires a kind of surrender or letting go. It is not really a matter of willpower. Instead, we must deflate our egos, accepting that we cannot dictate our future or change the past, that things do not always go the way they should. That "letting go" helps us embrace our life adventure with open-mindedness, courage, and hope. It is an unknown adventure, where we can learn new lessons and continue to grow. As I have hinted at and will discuss later, I like to think this surrender is a kind of spirituality, similar to what others experience in turning their life over "to the hands of God".

So we have a program that aims to change who you are on the inside, teaches principles that are spiritual in nature, and which has a core process of surrender or letting go. It is not about material success, but how one really lives.

For most, living by these spiritual principles is a brand new way of living. The result is not only a sense of freedom from self-centered chains about what I want or deserve, but also a renewed sense of self-value and serenity, which can nourish a sense of spirituality. At the same time it is not about seclusion – one remains involved in the world, seeking to make the world a better place without expecting anything back. This means we don't let it get to us when even our best efforts fail. We learn and move on, not living in resentment or fear, choosing acceptance, hope, and courage. We choose honesty, we shine light and love the best we can, and open ourselves to an unknown adventure of life. In the end these basic principles cultivate a positive, loving, and wholesome sense of being - what I simply call spiritual health.

Chapter 3

MY PERSONAL EXPERIENCE, STRENGTH, AND HOPE

Breakdown

August 9, 2010 my world collapsed. A text message was sent to me, and I dropped to the floor. I cried hysterically, in utter shock. The events which unfolded that day and the next few left me with no sense of reality. It turns out my wife was living a double life, one of addiction and infidelity. I always knew she was a "party girl" but this was much more. Friends and family were shocked. My wife left a few days later – she decided to enroll in a 30 day in-patient rehabilitation facility.

I was tormented by my emotions. They controlled me, in fact they owned me, defined me. The strongest emotion was anger. I wasn't just mad. I was filled with rage. I fantasized about killing certain people (those who had screwed me over), beating them into a pulp with my bare hands. But it was much more than that. Anger completely consumed me. I couldn't sleep, I was not even tired. Instead, I stayed up at night, closed myself in a room and yelled profanities, pummeling couch pillows and other things. Now I'm thankful the only real damage I did was one broken window, which a flying cardboard box hit. For weeks I slept only 2 hours per night or so, and I never was tired. My friends told me I needed to sleep, and I understood their point, but I was filled with too much rage.

In addition to no sleep, there was also no way I could work. My job requires me to think, and I could not concentrate on anything. People would ask me to solve certain problems, and I could no longer help them. I couldn't even start to help. There was simply no way I could focus on anything, except my emotions. I was mentally useless. I did what I could at work like answering simple emails, but I was mostly useless. Fortunately I had a great boss. I explained what was going on. He responded with understanding and encouragement, and gave me time to recover.

Another emotion that controlled me was pity. First off, everyone gave me lots of pity. They all felt sorry for me, even my wife's family and friends. But I was also full of self-pity. My life seemed meaningless. I didn't even care if I lived. Maybe I could save someone from a fire or something, and if I died in the process, well that's OK. At least I wanted to make my potential death useful, maybe like the movie Seven Pounds. Normally I loved playing golf, and now that I couldn't work, I had opportunities. But I didn't golf once. In fact I didn't golf until next summer. I just didn't care. I was a victim wallowing in self-pity, feeling that life was so unfair, so cruel.

I had a calendar on the wall, and I crossed out each day. I wasn't really living; I was just surviving each day. Someday, maybe I would be better. But I really had no idea what my life was going to be like. More than anything, I wanted a crystal ball. I wanted to know what would happen if I divorced my wife or if we stuck it out. I wanted to know who she was going to be after rehab. I wanted the crystal ball to see the future, but also to know what was really going on in her mind, and what she was going to do. Did she even love me? She said so, but maybe that was just a lie too. Maybe I was just a charity case and she said she loved me to make me feel better. I really had no idea who my wife was or what she thought of me. Reality was a complete unknown. The future was a complete unknown. Everything was lies, lies, lies. Then came the rage again.

So I lived with a raging resentment about what had been done to me. I lived in fear – not knowing what the future would be. I was also afraid of being a fool. Maybe my wife and her friends would all be laughing at me -- the idiot they could lie to, manipulate, and I would still be there. The thought of that brought raging anger.

Fortunately, I belonged to a gym and worked out. I ran and I pounded my body via weightlifting. The good news is that I got much stronger – I was almost worried about hurting myself. I will say that resentment brings with it an amazing energy. There is no doubt about the power of Darth Vader. I worked out trying to relieve the resentment inside me, work it out of my system, but no matter how hard I tried, the rage burned within me.

I didn't tell my family anything. I wasn't ready to talk to them yet. I felt ashamed of myself. I had been pushed around, manipulated, and felt like I was a failure. None of this would happen to a good husband, or so I thought. So I must be a complete loser. It would be a few months before I could move beyond thinking of myself as a failure and finally talk to my family.

I didn't drink during this time as I'm not an alcoholic. But I hit an emotional bottom. My life seemed completely hollow, meaningless. One afternoon, I was alone, and started sinking into self-pity. Tears took over, and grew with a mix of rage. It became uncontrollable. Anxiety mounted. I collapsed on the floor near the kitchen, completely consumed by resentment and fear. They had wrapped me in a web of self-pity, and I had lost any sense of who I was. I wanted to call someone for help, but

I didn't have a phone nearby and I didn't know who I could call. Not my family. Maybe the loonie police. I just couldn't think. I started rocking myself, saying "I can't live this way" over and over, and that is the last I remember. Later I woke up. But I knew I had to do something. My life was unmanageable, a complete mess.

My Normal Life

Before the events of August 2010 I just described, most people would probably have considered me a successful person. In fact, I'd likely be called an overachiever. Growing up I did great in school and I was even pretty good in sports. I didn't get into any real trouble. I put myself through school, graduated college with two bachelor degrees, honors and special distinctions. I earned an MA at Berkeley and a PhD at the University of Minnesota.

In the corporate world I was successful too, frequently promoted and considered a great employee. I worked up the corporate ladder, earned more money, helped buy a nice house, with a wife and two kids. My wife eventually left the workforce and became an at home mom, but I still helped with cooking, cleaning, and shopping. I thought my wife was beautiful, and I went out of my way to help her as much as I could, and be an attentive husband. I thought I was a pretty good husband and dad. I loved playing with the kids. I loved adventure, travel, and spending time with my family. Before the meltdown, I thought I was a success story. Surely my wife must be glad to have such a wonderful husband.

Yeah I was wonderful in many ways, which reminds me that I was also arrogant. I was probably stronger than you, faster than you, and almost certainly smarter than you. To top it all off, I was also a harder worker than you, with more discipline than you. I had put myself through college, working sometimes 40 hour weeks or more. I didn't really think my arrogance was a problem – it just went with my drive and my success.

Of course, my arrogance also meant I didn't really respect most people. They were undisciplined wimps. I didn't go around telling people this (at least not too much), but it showed in my actions. During recovery, I realized it really showed up in how I treated my wife. She was a party girl, and I didn't respect partiers. They weren't very productive, messed up responsibilities, and spent lots of money and time partying. When I was young none of this mattered much. My wife's partying provided comic relief, and was a source of entertainment. She was fun to watch and later we could tell funny stories about how she passed out at the bar with her hair in her beer.

But when we had kids, a house, and more responsibilities, it was no longer fun. I spent a lot of nights going to bed alone, fixing dinner with no one to show up, and feeling like I was second to partying. Resentment and a lack of respect developed. I'm not sure I understood then just how prevalent these attitudes were. It was only after my breakdown and subsequent reflection on resentment that I began to realize just how much resentment I had toward my wife and toward many other things. I won't go on about these other resentments. But like most of us I had resentments towards people who had screwed me over in the past, and general resentments that life had really treated me unfairly. I would even go so far as to say that much of my identity was defined by my resentments. I was proud of them, a badge of scars I had earned.

So in my "normal life" I was arrogant (as well I should be), I didn't respect others (and they didn't deserve it), and I held resentments (but who doesn't). But perhaps the most defining characteristic was that I wanted, perhaps craved, the praise of others. It was the praise of others that made me feel good. So my actions were often those of someone who was nice and supportive, even toward my partying wife who I didn't respect. I wanted praise from my parents, my teachers, my coworkers, my wife and kids. Of course that helped me be an overachiever. I wanted to be the best son, best husband, best father, smartest student, hardest worker. In any competition I wanted to win. These aren't bad in themselves, but why did I want these things? Because in return I wanted your praise. Your praise fed my ego and I was happy.

Looking outside oneself for happiness is what I call co-dependency. In my case, much of it came from the praise of others. We call this other-esteem, rather than self-esteem. I was very successful at other-esteem. Of course, if you didn't give me praise, or even worst criticized me, well then you were probably a stupid spineless wimp and added to my list of resentments. To be honest, I was not really aware that I lived this way at the time. It was not until recovery that I realized just how much resentment I carried around with me, and how much I really viewed myself as a victim and martyr seeking other-esteem.

When I first read Sartre's play *No Exit*, I was awestruck by how clearly it showed this dilemma of seeking praise. Even then (in high school), I recognized myself so clearly in those pages. I made the mistake of thinking the characters described not just my condition, or that of co-dependency, but the human condition. So I simply owned it. Yes I seek praise, that is what we all do, and for the disciplined it's what makes us successful. It would take the traumatic events of August 2010 (30 years after reading *No Exit*) before my normal life would be questioned, and I would begin to change.

Seeds of Change

Change was slow for me. Don't get me wrong there were a few spikes – "a ha" days that I will describe below. But I was not just magically healed one day by a shining light. It was a gradual unfolding for me.

I owe so much to The Retreat in MN (www.theretreat.org). This recovery facility is where my wife stayed for her month long rehabilitation. Part of my wife's rehabilitation involved reading the Big Book. I remember when she called, about a week into rehab, filled with excitement and told me the "Big Book" was her new handbook for living. I did not say anything, but rolled my eyes and thought – "oh God, another stupid self-help book filled with nonsense or trivial advice". Remember I was an arrogant intellectual. That said, over the next few weeks my wife did seem like she really was changing.

The Retreat is also where I attended a 3-day weekend family program. This was my introduction to the 12 step program. Leaders of the program gave me this so called "Big Book", parts of which we were going to read over the weekend. I figured I might as well get familiar with the crap my wife was reading in rehab.

At night in the Family Program we did a "tenth step", asking whether we were resentful, selfish, dishonest, or afraid (BB 86, paragraph quoted in first chapter). I admitted to all these defects, except dishonesty. But so what? I was entitled to resentment, damn it. I wanted to kill people, so I thought I was doing pretty damn good just keeping it to resentment. And who wouldn't be afraid in this situation? I had no idea what my life was going to be like. Who wouldn't be preoccupied with themselves, given all this crap? Finally, this Big Book was written for alcoholics, not me. So I didn't really care about failing the tenth step. Maybe my wife should care. But it did start my thinking about resentment, fear, and self-centeredness.

My wife and I both changed a lot from our time at the Retreat. I would like to tell people that when my wife came out of rehab and I came out of the family program that we were both healed. But it was really just the first surgery, a major surgery, with a long road of recovery ahead. For me, it was an invitation to question how I should live. I should also note that it was here where I first heard, from a guest speaker, about how his Higher Power was the principles of AA.

I continued to read the Big Book, mostly to understand what my wife should do to stay sober. I read it to gain insights about the alcoholic and what they had to do, but didn't really think most of it applied to me. I did come to understand that if I was really going to try my best to make our marriage work, resentment toward my wife had to go. Even if my resentment was more buried than visible, I knew my anger would come out sideways in little comments or mean jabs, and that would not help our marriage. But I had no intention to give up any other resentments (besides those toward my wife). For months I had dreams of revenge, both asleep and awake. I continued to wake up most nights from anger dreams. I was so entitled to resentment, even if it was bad for me.

Perhaps my biggest problem continued to be fear. I wanted a guarantee that if I tried my hardest at our marriage that it would work. I wanted to know that all this effort I was putting into our marriage was not just a waste of time, or worst just one big lie with me as the fool. I told my wife that I could forgive the past if I can have the future. But she said in all honesty that she could not make guarantees, only a commitment to really trying. We struggled with this a lot. I didn't think trying was enough. I was not ready to just try my best and still possibly lose.

One of the next important steps in my recovery was attending a Big Book study with my wife (website information: into-action.com). Nearly 200 people gathered for two hours every Sunday night for several months. An expert panel of four leaders in the AA community read each word of the Big Book and offered their comments. They provided amazing insight into the Big Book, the program of AA, and the nature of recovery. The class was so insightful that my wife and I took it a second time, to really understand the material well.

I learned so much from the Big Book seminar each week, and it deepened my understanding of recovery tremendously. Much of what I wrote in chapter two is a development of what I took away from this seminar. For me, one of the most pivotal moments in the seminar (and in my recovery) came when we talked about humility. For this, we read chapter 7 of the *Twelve Steps and Twelve Traditions*.

Up to this point, I clearly lacked humility, and I was fine with that. I thought humility was for losers, people who had failed or lacked confidence. But now for the first time I thought about humility as an actual virtue. It is not all about me and what I deserve, it's not about filling my agenda, it's not about what I achieve, it's not about feeding my ego with praise. This was the ego deflation, the surrender of self-centeredness that I had not understood. Now I saw how I was indeed self-centered in this most fundamental way. All that talk about self-centeredness that I dismissed also applied to me, not just my wife and alcoholics. I finally understood what people meant by "letting go". I had to let go of what I think I deserved in the past or I should have in the future. I needed to let go of resentment and fear, to learn from the past and be open-minded about the future. I saw how this seeking of humility was the "avenue to true freedom of the human spirit".

Of course it is easier to let go when you hit rock bottom or at least somewhere low. My dream of how my life would be was completely shattered. I thought I would be the best husband and we would have a nice family like "Little House on the Prairie", but with more money. In recovery, I gave up thinking about what I deserved, or even what might happen. I learned to focus on just my role: who I was and how I would live. I could control how I lived, and could influence others by my words and actions, but I could not dictate outcomes.

So I still tried to be the best husband I could be, to do all I could to help my wife be sober, to be the best father I could, and to be the best person I could. But humility means what actually happens beyond that is unknown. Maybe my efforts would fail, and my wife would lapse into addiction. To quote al-anon, I didn't cause my wife's alcoholism, and I can't control or cure it. Humility meant I had to accept that failure was possible. Failure did not mean I was a lousy husband or that I was an idiotic fool for even trying. Humility meant I gave up worrying about what others would think of my choices and the outcome, about whether they praised me or thought I was a fool. I was just going to try, not knowing what would happen, realizing that I would probably make mistakes, and that I was willing to be open to wherever the journey of life would take me.

This was an enormous step to take. But once I adopted this perspective, I really felt free. I was not responsible for the outcome, just trying. Failure was OK, as long as I tried my best. I really opened myself to whatever might happen. I would just focus on learning and developing my new found way of life. Relationships became a place for me to practice living by spiritual principles, to grow, and to learn to respond to others from a place of love and help. Whether I was successful or whether they praised me did not matter.

A key component of my recovery journey was the people I met, and what they showed me. I met many recovered alcoholics who were really amazing people. These people at one time might have been described as "scum of the earth". Some had been in prison, some stole money, some betrayed loved ones, many lied to get what they wanted. Selfish dishonesty was rampant. And now to meet these amazing people who turned their lives around, and became real role models, people who you would trust with your life, and cared so very much for everyone. It was really eye opening to meet these people. I had the good fortune to meet some of these role models during the family program at the Retreat, the panel in the Big Book group, and in various meetings.

My wife played a very big role in my recovery. Perhaps the most amazing thing is that she let me join her in her recovery. Of course, we needed our own space, but we also jointly attended some meetings. And more importantly we discussed our recovery with each other. We talked about our fears, our resentments, our self-pity, our feelings of loss, our regrets, our struggles. We talked about how to live this new life – how the spiritual principles applied to our daily life. We did it openly, honestly, and with respect for each other. Pia Mellody's book, *The Intimacy Factor* gave us excellent insight into how to do this. Our shared recovery became a basis for building intimacy.

One of the key things is that we both wanted each other to get better. From my point of view, it meant I had to put my wife's recovery ahead of my selfish interests. It was not about me making her into the person I thought she should be. It was about me helping her to build her own recovery and life her way. It also meant ultimately that her recovery might lead her to reject us as a couple. I had to accept that possibility. Even though I had "taken her back", learned about recovery, given up resentment, treated her with respect, and nourished her the best I could, our relationship might still end. My life was less about preserving our relationship, than having us both grow in recovery, and see where that goes. Developing this attitude took a long time. I wanted guarantees, remember. Instead, I had to really learn a new attitude of open-mindedness toward the future.

One day I remember imagining that a magic fairy appeared to me when I was young – the night before my wedding. The fairy had a crystal ball and showed me all the key events that would happen in my marriage. At the end the crystal ball showed me how my world would crumble during August 2010, with my wife in rehab and me laying on the floor in tears.

If I had seen all this in the crystal ball on the night before my wedding day, I would have left my fiancée at the altar. I would have thanked the magic fairy for saving me from a terrible decision to marry this woman and have a miserable future. I would have gladly chosen another life.

But now that I think about it, I don't know what my other life (without my current wife) would have been. I wish I could say I would have learned the lessons of humility, of letting go of resentments and fears, of practicing rigorous honesty. But it's doubtful. There's a very good chance that the fairy's crystal ball would have led me to a life without the happiness, without the tools for living that I now have. So while the crystal ball would have led me to run from my wedding day like the plague, I can truly say now that I'm grateful for the life I have lived. Sure my life has had its tragic moments, and good moments too, but I feel so blessed to have learned the lessons I did, and become the person I am now. For me, recovery opened a door to a new way of life.

My life today is much richer and satisfying than ever before. By this, I don't mean that everything is smooth sailing. I actually have lots of new challenges in my life. Many would say they are even bigger problems than the one with my wife, which triggered my recovery journey. But the difference now is that the inside of me, who I am and how I respond to life, is so much better. I still experience anger and fear, but they are emotions that come and go - I don't live in fear and resentment. I have a much healthier perspective on my life, how I want to live, and how I want to respond to life's events.

It's made a big difference in how I live, in my ordinary days, during the beautiful times, and when things don't go right.

When people used to ask me the common question, "How are you?" I would look at my outside circumstances. I was a consumer of happiness. If things were going well, then I was happy. Of course, I could usually find something that was not quite right and complain – especially living in MN where the weather is often undesirable for me. But now I don't let the outside world, my external life situation, define me. I can choose my attitude, I can try to change things, and I can accept what I cannot change. "How are you?" is now a question about who I am and how I choose to respond to life's events.

Ever since I was a teenager I parroted the common proverb that "life is a journey, not a destination". But now I have a much deeper understanding of what that means, and I really live that way. I feel a real sense of freedom and serenity. Before all this, I never knew how unsatisfactory my normal life really was. Of course, I sometimes slip into old habits. Some days I wake up feeling kind of flat. Sometimes I still seek praise, and sometimes I am arrogant. These are just a few of my defects. So I am far from perfect. But I have a new direction, a new plan for my life, with a much healthier perspective, along with better attitudes, motives, and behaviors. My life really is much richer and satisfying than *My Normal Life* before.

My aim in this section was to share my experience, strength, and hope, just as others do in recovery. I hope to have also sprinkled a little laughter. For surely there is insight in Victor Hugo's quip that "Laughter is the sun that drives winter from the human face." Perhaps my story and its lessons will help some lost souls, or help my children live a better life. I hope they can learn these lessons easier than I did. Unfortunately it seems most of us learn things the hard way.

Chapter 4

PHILOSOPHICAL REFLECTIONS ON HUMILITY, WITH AND WITHOUT GOD

Bowing down before God, thanking Him for the life we have, asking Him for help to make ourselves better and to guide us, accepting ourselves as fallible servants of His will, living the kind of life He wants us to live. I like these images – they are powerful, touching, and instructive ideas about a spirituality rooted in a truly deep humility, what I call true humility.

But for some, these ideas about God are not effective. I have many friends who don't believe in God - who are atheists. I mention this because my intent with this book is to write something that would still be useful to them, as well as people in recovery who are agnostic or atheist. This is one reason I have focused on the basic principles of recovery, and not brought God in, except to add instructive insight.

It is also probably time for me to be honest and reveal that I am most likely an agnostic or very liberal theist. I have no bond to any specific organized religion. That said, I was raised Christian, but broke from mainstream Christianity in my youth. I do not hold the Bible as the word of God. I'm even troubled by some of it – like God punishing people by killing their firstborn children, or telling Moses to kill the male children and non-virgin women of Midianite enemies or even the mass genocide that is Noah's Ark. I also never understood the basic idea of atonement in Christianity. I simply don't understand why Christ apparently had to die on the cross in order to save us. Why can't God just decide to forgive us? How does blood sacrifice of an innocent bring salvation? That said, I've always liked the teachings of Jesus, and consider him a great role model. I just disagree with typical Christian theology, and to be honest I think much of it may be historical reconstruction which even Jesus would perhaps disagree with.

Recovery is neutral on these religious issues. It shifts the focus to a "God of your understanding". As a philosopher some of my key thoughts about God have been influenced by the problem of evil. Why does God (if He is all powerful) allow so much suffering and pain? One can say God allows people free will, but that response only goes so far. With God's power the gun about to kill innocent children could be jammed or melt, or the bullets could dissolve. God could disable an airplane's controls, and lock them on autopilot to prevent 911. And beyond the evil people do, what about natural evil? Why did God allow an earthquake to kill 40,000 people most of whom were gathered in Churches on All Saints Day?

I realize that we all need challenges to grow, and I completely agree that suffering has a larger purpose in developing our potential. But I question the degree to which an omnipotent God's moral decisions allow such severe brutality, torture, and crippling disasters when he could stop them. I know I need to let my children learn from mistakes and that suffering builds character, but I also know that I would do anything to prevent them from being kidnapped and tortured, or massacred at a school shooting. That is more suffering than anyone needs to grow. As hard as I try, I cannot ignore that if God is truly active, benevolent and all powerful then the world would be a different place.

This is my position. The old Kevin would have argued until

you agreed or ran away and hid. Now I'm just explaining what I have to work with. For me, God has at best limited powers, or at least chooses to act so. Perhaps He is more like a human father or mother, wishing the best for his children, but lacking the power to protect them. Or maybe His power is limited to working within us when we truly seek to change ourselves, perhaps when we ask Him or let go of our self-centeredness.

While I've expressed my doubts about God's power, I think what ultimately matters is the underlying way of living, of being. Those who live as true disciples of a loving omnipotent God can provide a wonderful model of this way of life. But I think one can live this same way even if one thinks God has limited power, or does not even exist. In the first chapter I outlined how this looks. Accepting what we cannot change, letting go of resentments, being open-minded about the future, doing our best and accepting that the outcome is uncertain, rigorous honesty, and asking what we can do to help the world.

Fundamental to this way of living is ego deflation, the surrender of self-centeredness, humility. This ego deflation is less about willpower than learning a new way of life. Indeed, having more willpower can actually make ego deflation harder. We can get used to control, to success. It becomes more difficult to accept that we cannot dictate the outcome, we cannot make people into who we want them to be, we can't guarantee things will work out. Learning the new way of life involves learning acceptance, learning to let go of what I deserve, learning open-mindedness. Of course, willingness or wishing to learn this new way of life is a start, coupled with responsible effort, honesty, and accountability. But it's also a change in my heart, my soul, my way of being.

Viewing ourselves as disciples of a loving omnipotent God makes humility easier. As God's devoted servants, praying for his help and guidance, we assume some humility. In addition, we gain comfort from believing God is in control. If we think

God has limited or no power, there is no assurance of God orchestrating a divine plan – there to watch our back, ensure divine justice, or guarantee us a better future, in heaven or on earth. Without God's omnipotence, learning how to live in courage, and letting go of fear, is more difficult.

Given the historical influence of the Christian based Oxford Group on AA, it is not surprising that the idea of serving a loving almighty God would become the primary context in which ego deflation and letting go of self-centeredness was described and developed. But reducing self-centeredness is also common to many Eastern spiritual traditions.

One of the most radical suggestions, popular in the West, is that there is no ego at all. The ego, "your distinct self", is an illusion. There is just one big universe that we have interpreted as having individuals – we impose duality. When I was young I thought the idea of "no-self" was rebellious and cool. I told many this is what I believed - in high school I labeled myself an Existentialist Zen Buddhist. But despite my best efforts, deep down I never could really believe in "no-self". I won't argue the point here, but note that for many people this worldview is highly counter intuitive. I also think it raises difficult questions about freedom, personal responsibility, and morality.

A more moderate view of ego deflation that I favor can be found in many interpretations of Taoism. Taoism involves surrendering, letting go, and following The Way. This letting go of our self-centeredness, which I call humility, is one of the three treasures/virtues of Taoism (along with compassion/love and simplicity).

One of my favorite passages from the *Tao Te Ching* is: "Know Honor, Yet Keep Humility (Chap. 28)". I like this passage because it does not associate humility with weakness or worthlessness. We should know honor, toward ourselves and others. We should be strong servants of doing what is right.

But we should not become full of ourselves, inflating our ego. Yes, we need to know honor, yet remain humble.

There is in this process a kind of balancing. I don't think the Yin/Yang balancing applies to everything. But I think for instance there is a balance between "trying" vs. "acceptance /open-mindedness/surrender". I grew up wanting to change the world and fight for my dreams, and I still think this is very noble. But at the same time, one must be open-minded about what happens in life and sometimes adapt. So there is a kind of balance in trying our best to influence what happens, but sometimes accepting a different outcome.

Likewise, nurturing is a balance between helping too little (or none) and helping too much help (enabling). Helping others also has to be balanced with time and care for ourselves. Helping others should not come from playing the role of martyr or from feeling we are worthless. We want to honor ourselves <u>and</u> others. On the flip side, we should not take our honor, our helping of others, our belief in ourselves as a means to building big egos. Again, there is a balance – we want a strength that is humble. What we want is true humility.

True humility is a positive form of ego-deflation. It recognizes our fallibility, and that others make mistakes too. We accept that we influence outcomes, but we are not omnipotent Gods who can dictate outcomes. Humility allows us to let go of resentments about what I deserved in the past and fears about what I will have in the future. It puts aside my demands on life, and opens myself to the journey of life that unfolds. Humility helps us to admit and amend our wrongs. It takes us from takers to genuine givers who expect nothing back, from asking "what can the world do for me" to "what can I do to make the world a better place"?

This humility can be further deepened in many ways. For instance, I stand in awe before the fascinating and complex structure of our universe. I am amazed at the mystery of life itself and the remarkable lives of animals. I believe in free will, but have no idea where it comes from or how it works. So I agree with Shakespeare: "There are more things in heaven and earth than dreamt of in your philosophy". This sense of wonder and awe is something I use to ground me, to bring me back to humility and deepen it. It is easy for me to stray from this humility as I am so used to feeding my ego and praising myself for all that I know. Humility is a practice I continue to learn, better understand, and grow within myself.

In the end, my faith is in the power of living by the spiritual principles I have discussed. When people in recovery ask me about my Higher Power, I tell them it is the spiritual principles discussed here, perhaps coupled with the community of recovery, and the help of others. The texts of AA are filled with references to "spiritual principles" that one should live by, and it is these principles I have tried to clarify here. The foundation of these principles is humility.

> Indeed, the attainment of greater humility is the foundation principle of each of A.A.'s Twelve Steps (12&12, pg. 70)

I believe that living by these principles is the way to a glorious life. It does not mean that I will have financial security, that my loved ones will be happy, or that others will think wonderful things of me. It does not mean any specific life situation will occur or even that I will get into heaven. It's not about the outcome, but who we are.

As a philosopher I take the principles of 12 step recovery to be a significant contribution to what philosophers call "virtue ethics". Without getting into much detail, virtue ethics stresses living the kind of life a "virtuous person" would. It is about being virtuous, not achieving specific outcomes (utilitarianism) or obeying certain rules (deontological ethics). When I first read Aristotle, who founded virtue ethics, I thought of this virtuous person as a self-righteous do-gooder who thought highly of themselves and would lecture me on my faults. But now I think of this person as much more humble. Someone who makes mistakes, recognizes their own fallibility, and grasps the uncertainty in life. Someone who has suffered and learned to accept that suffering as part of life, and grown from it. Someone who has learned to let go of resentment and fear. Someone who really cares about others, respects them, tries to understand them, wishes the best for all and has the courage to love without expecting anything in return.

One of the most provocative claims Aristotle made is that a virtuous life is something we pursue to live well, to thrive. Many of us think living a virtuous life is something we have to do, perhaps to get to heaven, or because it's what others expect, or because we will be punished otherwise. But for Aristotle, living a virtuous life is fundamental to flourishing as a human being. This is the same lesson we learn in recovery.

Living by spiritual principles is a new framework for living well. To really work it must be something we want to do, not out of obligation or submission, but because it is the way to a better life. And it must become a real practice, something we work on, maintain, grow, and live by. "The spiritual life is not a theory. *We have to live it.*" (BB 83)

Unfortunately, it is all too easy to follow in Darth Vader's footsteps. Wrapped in resentment and fear, his big ego drove him into the dark side. Maybe darkness does not consume us like Darth Vader, but we live, sometimes unknowingly, in a shroud of darkness. We imprison ourselves with fear, resentment, self-centeredness, and dishonesty. They may feel like familiar friends, maybe even feel like they define us. But they are chains that imprison us in darkness. Letting go of these chains brings us from the darkness of prison toward the light that is "true freedom of the human spirit".

The Indigo Girls in their classic song *Closer to Fine* describe the contrast between dark and light this way:

Well darkness has a hunger that's insatiable
And lightness has a call that's hard to hear

Darkness has a hunger that can never be satisfied. There is always more to have, more to control, more to resent. Darkness also has a call that is easy to hear, easy to follow. There is no shortage of disappointment, heart break, and injustice. It is all too easy to respond with resentment and fear that we know so well, and drive ourselves deeper into self-centeredness. We can even completely close ourselves to the light, as Darth Vader did. It was only near the end of his life, watching his innocent son being murdered that Darth Vader realized what he had become, and remembered the hero he used to be.

For many of us it takes these rock-bottom moments to finally hear the call to lightness. By letting go of our self-centeredness, our resentments and fears, we free ourselves from chains of darkness and liberate the light within us. And with a little help from honesty, gratitude, hope, love and the way of life we have described, that light within us may grow stronger and shine ever brighter.

Some have told me that by letting go of my self-centeredness and living by spiritual principles that I let God into my life, whether I know it or not. I think this is a beautiful idea, both poetic and powerful. It makes me smile. Perhaps this less powerful God is like a Holy Spirit, a Spirit of Divine Love, or Tao that pervades the universe. Perhaps we can let this "spirit of light" into our lives as we let go of darkness, and truly seek a new life. Of course, I really don't know whether this is true, but I'm humble enough to know that my knowledge is limited and accept the possibility.

Made in the USA
Columbia, SC
16 October 2020

22909372R00033